Theater of Animals

Theater of Animals

Poems by
Samn Stockwell

University of Illinois Press   Urbana and Chicago

This book is printed on acid-free paper.

"Poem of My Father" (formerly "Prologue") and "April in the Village"
previously appeared in *The New Yorker*.
"Aphrodite at Solstice" and "The Tomb of the Wrestlers"
previously appeared in *New Letters Review*.

Library of Congress Cataloging-in-Publication Data

Stockwell, Samn.
    Theater of animals : poems / by Samn Stockwell.
        p.   cm. — (National poetry series)
    ISBN 0-252-06476-3 (pbk.)
    I. Title. II. Series.
PS3569.T615T48   1995
811'.54—dc20   94-46117
                                                        CIP

The National Poetry Series

The National Poetry Series was established in 1978 to publish five collections of poetry annually through five participating publishers. The manuscripts are selected by five poets of national reputation. Publication is funded by James A. Michener, The Copernicus Society of America, Edward J. Piszek, The Lannan Foundation, The National Endowment of the Arts, The Tiny Tiger Foundation, and The Echoing Green Foundation.

1994 Competition Winners

Erin Belieu, *Infanta*
Selected by Hayden Carruth, published by Copper Canyon Press

Pam Rehm, *To Give It Up*
Selected by Barbara Guest, published by Sun and Moon Press

Matthew Rohrer, *A Hummock in the Malookas*
Selected by Mary Oliver, published by W. W. Norton

Samn Stockwell, *Theater of Animals*
Selected by Louise Glück, published by the University of
  Illinois Press

Elizabeth Willis, *The Human Abstract*
Selected by Ann Lauterbach, published by Viking Penguin Press

For Beth

With thanks to Jackie Rae

Contents

3

1

The Train

Here, on the train
a face waits,
the thin jaw
leaning on the glass
when a hand reaches
to touch the lip.

It waits for you,
something, sorrow
to remove its dull eye
from the great darkness.

The world opens up
and abandons, abandons.

Poem of My Father

1.

It is night,
my father is running.
My mother is gathering laundry
sweeping across the yard
with long white arms.

We are moving.
Kneeling in the back seat,
I stare through the window.
Some man, wearing an old cap,
clutches a cane
in front of his barn. Then
wood by the road's edge,
crumbling to ash.

My mother sits on the lawn,
intent on the pocket
of her orange dress. My father,
sipping bourbon, berates us.
It will take all afternoon
to enter the doorway.

2.

My father is a gray man,
there's mold in his teacup.
On Sunday he climbs the ladder
to clean the roof's gutter.
My father watches the smoke of bacon
seep through the window ledge.
He hears my grandfather
in the bedroom,
and in the living room,
the broom thrust over the carpet.

3.

There was more on the floor than now
seems possible: books and hard candy,
cardboard games with minute tin balls.
A pair of heavy boots broke everything
and the children were sprawled outside,
some limp, others spinning forever
over the sidewalk. Your father was calling;
another mother patted her hard hand on your cheek.
The swing broke, there was a root
under your chest, a man lifting
his heavy arms around you.

Harvest

The cat sings by the cornice,
the puddles fuse,
grass leans into cowlicks
in fields spotted with children.
Their mothers wait
like obelisks above the hill,
the long years weighting them.

The wind rushes in the gables
to cover the tenant's sigh.
The postman grates his hand
against his beard.

Field empty, their eyes
squeezed tight against sunlight,
the women turn,
they dream of the moon
lifting them out of their bedrooms,
leaving them thin as ribbons.

Curfew

A small boy draws a tree
that looks like a small
boy with uncombed hair.
Then he draws a witch
grasping with some vigor
a broomstick. He owns
a coat of armor and
a secret animal. Near
the sidewalk,
girls hurl themselves
through stinging ropes.
But why is he always fleeing
too late from the girls he has struck
and never reaching
home before his father's anger?

Poem after N.G.

Years ago a woman wore a yellow dress;
rain the color of rust
touched the screen door.
Impatiens surrounded the steps.
Seasons waited
and the sound of a gray piano
filled the arbor.

Wearing a long coat,
she crosses the room. Her child,
who feels she is a horse,
follows in a violet jacket.

They want to enter the hall
where someone is carving white birds.
Behind the thick walls,
the child heard them rising.

The Difficult Years

My mother sits in the bathtub,
cutting away. Fiber swells out
of her arm. She feels the uselessness
of others and the severing edge
of time, but not the aging that accompanies
pain, or its reduction.

For My Sister

You can come out of the sand.
Someone will dance and no one
will tie your legs apart.

Held under, you grew very calm
and heavy. I'm sorry
I left you, with your throat tightening,
sitting squash-eyed on the stairs,
never to be sober.

Lease

I hang my lantern over
the river and swim
in the freezing stream,
ice at the back of my neck
and behind my eyes.

Once there was a strong man
who could lift nothing but
his weights. Neither a baby
in tears nor a dusty suitcase
askew in the attic
could he lift otherwise.

I want not to be
the teller of tales
or keeper of scales,
but to open my
wallet and pay.

At the Exhibit

Calder knew everything about animals.

My aunt is baking rolls
when the exhibit closes,
beside the room where my dead cousins
were lifted through the window.

I brought a young woman
to dinner who lifts my face
with kisses.

Who will help my cousins to finish
their lesson when my aunt is turning
the seams, and the felted
umber of dry earth stretches
over the lawn?

Incest

Think of that old man, who has enough stones
in his memory to make all his clothes runneled
with flatulence. I expose this Christian before you,
proving he has lied and continues to violate neighborhood
    children:
who else would know this but someone who has traveled
a great distance, and is not a native?
Think, when you are sick afterward, and salt
has made a thick case of your tongue.
Mother is in the dining room, miserable
over a recent painting, and the air smells like kerosene
and laundry. All the young cousins are bent over their card
    game.
Nobody speaks until dinner, eager to go into the streets
and for the story someone will tell, over beer, in the late
    hours.

Vincent's Story

—Arles

And for a long time, sheared wood
and the pockets under the eyes pinching blood—
What a story, to sweat and then
sleep on the grass hearing the blades
swing in their sockets as the machine nears.
A tiny man weeping into his shoes. Trucks
are carrying blocks the size of cottages.
Furthermore, everyone is running from him.
His aunt is whispering, "Spider's egg, spider's egg."

He turns toward Gauguin, then back.
Outside the café a doctor is waiting
and Theodore—to go home, wrapped
in their wooden arms, where the earth
cracks at the doorstep.

Memorial for the Dead Brother

In later years, reason is like
a vise. The comparison that was
my regret, my downfall, never becomes
a memory. I feel the constancy
of exertion and, in exertion, I think
of death so vibrant and elastic,
to make real people of my family.

From Burr Creek

As the sea has two green lines
to clear it away from the sky,
the morning smokes briefly
while the ground pulls to the sun.

Nothing gradual in sleep. Who would
think it takes years to bring such decline?
It's autumn; the leaves peel out,
wrapped in the dust of old stems.
Cliff of decay; memory when climbed
with terror.

Night of its darkness,
sky with winter's stars.

2

Dictionary of the Theater

The cat squeezes
its fife notes
over the actors.

On such notes, closure
as well as silence.

The actors bow their heads.

They are not one reed against age,
one spark among the slight embers.

They lie in the meadow and the fat bulbs
of the earth are live hands among them.

The Actors

The lawyer, smoothing her red skirt,
taps her fingers on the window.
The theater is starting.
Programs are turned in the still air
and a wall of swelled clothes and jewelry opens.

Lamps are put on in the outer office;
a custodian moves slowly down the corridor.
The streetlamps, at first weakly,
fill the sidewalk with orange.
She watches the leaves heaving in the branches
and unfolds the jacket across her shoulder.
In the long steps from curb to curb
the gray fans through her hair
like oil spreading over a light cloth.

She watched them cluttering the restaurant
in red cloaks and black gloves, but
one of them must have gone through the park
after sunset, and missed the one
who walked with her and read the newspaper
when she was tired.

Goddess of a Thousand Names

We step off
where there is no love.
Then we begin to count again.
We are here
to become smaller.

This longing is from
the dark that leaves.
Soon it will be spring.
In our dreams we hear
knives sharpening, skin
ticking against the bed.

Music

Telemann and Vivaldi lived in the same village.
The smoke from their chimneys mingled
in the scenic clouds. They blazed forth.

Vivaldi's wife, with too much chin
and too little bone, drew water
under a close replica of the yellow sun
we have today, as they tatted their songs.
Whole crowds paused, while the barriers
of meadow and forest opened.

April in the Village

It is so quiet in the afternoon;
you breathe or pause, and something
presses against your chest.

I read. On the bed
beside me, two women
make love.

There are thin round
crates of lemons.
Past the window,
a man is hauling
open boxes of lettuce and plums.

On the bed, someone cries
and is sucked out
of the breast.

A square of yard
is being swept.
The grasses begin to go out
around the lamppost.

Cat

What will the cat do
in my slipper? I have a black
kitten in a yellow slipper.
Black when the day ends.
Suppose a cast of greenness.

Who has covered the breakfast cake
with cornstarch?
Someone's fevered neck
is laid on the table.

The cat is in the cupboard, waving
her plumed tail through the shutter.
The monkey is in the lemon jar.
Munificence. Munificence and chaos.
How finely the carpenters dovetailed the stairs.

The cat is in the boot. The rug has saliva on it.

Five quarters to cover coffee and muffins
for a week. My black sandals,
which I believe I left by the pond,
are out at the heel.

Where is the cat now?

The cat is on the flagged walk.
The cat, in the pantry,
is tumbling figs on the floor.

The Band

Tomorrow, madness and the collective
voice shattered. Holed up in a chemical dead city
the cast thinks they have caught a terminal disease.
They crawl into the country; their shiny suits
jar against bland gardens. Here, the women
are like automatons, wound over their plots,
heaviness in all their movements. Poor children, to think
this is what is offered: sterility. Eating melon
in the immaculate park, sterility doesn't seem much
to complain of.

Never an Ax, Always a Saw

"You'll drive me to the grave."
Which today I wouldn't mind
so much, spooning the cool earth
over your furious body.
It's a nice day for a drive
and a little gardening, though
little of what you promise
comes true.

The Rake's Progress

. . . I am suffering. The next party
will not be as good as the last.
Maybe I should dress and go to the bar.

On the streets I see
a chorus of young boys.
Above them, by the open
window, a beautiful woman,
bathed in her spacious
lamplight, opening her robe
for me.

The Woolfs by Water

In the kitchen they bathed
in a small tub, tentatively resting
under the clouds of soap. Imagine
them otherwise; disembarking
from their gowns at a picnic;
the seclusion amid the fronds
as they dipped and sank beneath
the pond, the subaquatic realm
she was later to become so famous for.

Dancing

"And we were so awkward."
Too much art, not enough lies.
All that will ever come of this:
dust, dust, and longing.
Everything is so green beside
the debris of winter.
You've touched someone whose heart
is such a small dish, it overturned.

Aphrodite at Solstice

A bird in the tower of sky
and the exile
finds sea rocket growing.
The moonflower blooms;
one on the first night,
two on the second.

She returned through the water.
Just like Athena, miserably screeching
out of her father's head, this was torture.
There is no other home
for the body's longings.
The breast and the sea
are one ocean.

Stardust

The woman rocking as stiffly
as a pendulum, a band with two trombones
and a man grasping the waist of the woman
with no arms, and swinging her, laughing,
over the dance floor. Two small women
hold each other in the parking lot,
wings burst from their shoulders, pulling them
up, over the party, over the village.

Couples walk in the meadow, and the women
shrink in the sky, as though heaven were reclaiming
its own detritus.

3

Lazarus

Martha and Mary stood off
from Lazarus; there was no occupation
for him. Alders grew by the brook
where they washed the house
clean of its habitation. He knew
their dreams but was not of them.
Smelling like lilies, he followed Martha
throwing handfuls of gravel;
"Dream I am sweet, dream I am sweet."
No one could rest. The sight of his chest,
rising and falling . . . He fled
and returned to his burial cave
and lived as a great oracle,
blind to all ordinary events.

The Tomb of the Wrestlers

His wife poses on the balcony.
I cannot recall a modern painting
in which the human form has been recorded
with so much faith. The gradation
of the flushed cheek to blue, the dispirited
hand loosened from the post.

Roses climbing over
the banister; cakes in the oven
and smoke filling the room.

Night

The windows blacken
as though this is temporary.
In the shops are ceramic
animals that remind me
of our walk. The violent smell
of hibiscus, the ash color
of the walkway.

Red lights on the black night.
The warm light that comes between black shutters.
My girlfriend with splintery hands.
My hands that smelled of detergent, of summer.
The graceful fire escape at the back
of the hotel. And the bleak noise that followed us,
those lonesome people, always crowded
against a brown sky.

Something persistent gleams
out of a quartered sandlot. Down the street
a wedding party issues from a church.
The bride is downcast, and walks
sullenly along the sidewalk, kicking
the bright litter with her silver foot.

The difference between "bought" and "brought."
My puppy with such a short tail.
I want to fall in love again, but
without a garden, the roar of cushions
dropping, hitting the stricken mice.

Errand

Groaning the whole time?
As though pockets of ants
were pinned under the skin?
One short-fingered hand grabbed
each calf and stuffed them into
boots. Who heard them? It was wet,
the pavement slippery, the sun
going down, and the shops
closing their shutters.

The Café

The cook who has trundled
under baskets of greens
raises his shoulders and wishes
for a month by the ocean. He wants
to be as still and as pastel
as the couple who sit in their unhindered
silence by the engrossing wallpaper.

The couple turn to their fish
as the fantastically pained
turn to ritual.

The cook arches his eyebrows.
His feet ache and their bulbous reflection
on the polished cooler frightens him.
Each day he rises and is blinded
by his labor, like the sobering passion
of the perfectly unhappy couple, but
less solitary, without the revival of fear,
like this slow, caught moment in the afternoon.

Long Division

Misery is the museum left
from the real anguish of the moment.
Only the vaporish tongue, in its dream
movements, consoles, arranging love
like an altitude map of small
islands, the old volcanoes pushing
their magma through sleek oceans
like impartial fingers.

Easter

Before noon the chicory quits flowering
and the roadside is like a beach.
Swung from the arms of the boy, the residue
of the intestines slews out of the dead cat,
pummeling the dust. This violence
is insufficient, the way loneliness
is not enough to create love.

The eggs were pushing
through the ground.
You were next to me, a hand
on the sleepy forehead
but I was the only child.

Far along the streets
lined with daffodils, mothers
were carrying cakes and crosses
to the miniature churches. You
pulled my head between your breasts,
the voices of the women's choir
nearing on their long procession.

3.

I enter the house where there is no milk.
Is this when you think of Christ,
smelling soup from a nearby kitchen, imagining
the flecks of meat scraped from a plate?

Perhaps we are a memory to him also—
the way we stood in the cold streets
and felt a sweetness enter the air
like a season.

And of what do the seasons run empty?

4.

I believe I am healing,
not aging, lying so still
to all whispers in the air.
Age is the illness
of weakening, like a bird wrapped
beneath a great snowstorm.

I am harboring,
harboring a village
of youth within me.

Love Poem

—for Kathie

I'm glad it's another cool day
with potholes blossoming
toward summer. And you,
my pocket, beside me.
And the cherry trees
not in bloom, retreating
into their buds' huts.

As we advance into the mud,
it parts like a clay ocean.
Moses would have been proud.
He would have chirped, "Oh yes,
this is it, girls,
this is love."

V-Day

In Vienna, an old woman
digests a biscuit and her
left foot halts under
the frayed diagram of black
cloth. The strafed city
and sheered-off childhoods.
She turns her coat away
from the rescuers. Everything
salvageable is suspended
above the clouds, and all
that is left of brick will
continue to turn the color
of stone.

Four Memories

Yesterday I made a pot of soup
and watched the wall spot with tomato paste
above the brilliantly wired mixer.
I walked the streets by Yale,
lingering outside the British Museum,
waiting for the bars to open.
Poor consciousness, always rushed
beneath the silly patterned sky,
forever desiring a piece of toast,
a cup of tea.

The door opens and everyone enters,
the eyes in one immovable head
mist over and over. What a strain
to speak over the impassioned music
as couple after couple
careen onto the dance floor.

Contract

In my wool sweaters I imagine the countryside
lodged in a life of grating happiness.
Morning, I imagine the factory: large blue spaces
that smell of heavy oil, solitary men
eating dry sandwiches. It is better
than thinking of my return from work,
couples partaking of the same
petrified air, my breath in clouds
and the concentric waves of my shaking hands
rattling the locked door.

Should none of us worry the carpet?
The night full of small things
and the day smaller?

North Avenue

I hear the door of the oven
creaking and a pan shifting
and imagine the window broken
as though to let someone lean
into the street for repair
from the taunts of domesticity.
The rustle between summer
dress and satin shirt rises
through the deserted hall, the sound
that lifts above the larval
tenement and laboratory after
laboratory of its inhabitants.

Profile of the Ocean

The ocean is like a black sedan;
it makes us larger but featureless.

She has her hand cupped over my breast
and I have cold or transfixed thought
from which many are fleeing.

The extreme clatter of living
recedes like a woman gliding
into the night on foamy high heels.

If writing was a simple aggressive act
and not content emptying into injury
wouldn't it be easy to lift the huge bodies
of our compatriots from the water?

A Week

Don't go out to the orange trees til noon.
A grove of pianos and flutes rests beside the lonely dog.
The mat is full of babies and soft pretzels.

Who is standing where the bricks are falling down?
Someone who tends a garden of delphiniums.
The storekeeper moving the bottles to the stoop
has cracked his eyeglasses.
It is that cold, that cold.

For J.R.

The sky cleared briefly
and we could see the fisher
working the opposite rocks
and hear, "She never married,
she lives with a woman companion."

Phragmites billowing from the mouth
of the harbor; our secret duplicated.
Embarrassed to wave a soft persimmon
from its limb.

A memory shaped by scent, by the reluctant
fruit bursting on our doorstep.

Fear of Bridges

What am I thinking of?
I am thinking of presents.
In one version of this story
my friends arrive for an evening
of drinking. Finding me already
drunk, they send me to the bridge
factory where I lie on the high
arched frames and pretend
I am making a decision.

In another paragraph, I am
reclaimed by my loved one,
the chainmaker. Often
belief arises of escape
from the element
you were designed for.

Now I oil the casement,
then I fix the drains.

Mourner

Roads crumble but the walls remain.
I am the spring of chaos and God's string
runs from my anus to my head.

Few heard the man before this day
and none will hear him after.

Tiny life, blind
as a seed. Not a sound
escapes the gates of earth.

Stepping into emptiness,
I have learned to make music.

Illinois Poetry Series

Laurence Lieberman, Editor

History Is Your Own Heartbeat
Michael S. Harper (1971)

The Foreclosure
Richard Emil Braun (1972)

The Scrawny Sonnets and Other
Narratives
Robert Bagg (1973)

The Creation Frame
Phyllis Thompson (1973)

To All Appearances: Poems New
and Selected
Josephine Miles (1974)

The Black Hawk Songs
Michael Borich (1975)

Nightmare Begins Responsibility
Michael S. Harper (1975)

The Wichita Poems
Michael Van Walleghen (1975)

Images of Kin: New and Selected
Poems
Michael S. Harper (1977)

Poems of the Two Worlds
Frederick Morgan (1977)

Cumberland Station
Dave Smith (1977)

Tracking
Virginia R. Terris (1977)

Riversongs
Michael Anania (1978)

On Earth as It Is
Dan Masterson (1978)

Coming to Terms
Josephine Miles (1979)

Death Mother and Other Poems
Frederick Morgan (1979)

Goshawk, Antelope
Dave Smith (1979)

Local Men
James Whitehead (1979)

Searching the Drowned Man
Sydney Lea (1980)

With Akhmatova at the Black
Gates
Stephen Berg (1981)

Dream Flights
Dave Smith (1981)

More Trouble with the Obvious
Michael Van Walleghen (1981)

The American Book of the Dead
Jim Barnes (1982)

The Floating Candles
Sydney Lea (1982)

Northbook
Frederick Morgan (1982)

Collected Poems, 1930–83
Josephine Miles (1983)

The River Painter
Emily Grosholz (1984)

Healing Song for the Inner Ear
Michael S. Harper (1984)

The Passion of the Right-Angled
Man
T. R. Hummer (1984)

Dear John, Dear Coltrane
Michael S. Harper (1985)

Poems from the Sangamon
John Knoepfle (1985)

In It
Stephen Berg (1986)

The Ghosts of Who We Were
Phyllis Thompson (1986)

Moon in a Mason Jar
Robert Wrigley (1986)

Lower-Class Heresy
T. R. Hummer (1987)

Poems: New and Selected
Frederick Morgan (1987)

Furnace Harbor: A Rhapsody of
the North Country
Philip D. Church (1988)

Bad Girl, with Hawk
Nance Van Winckel (1988)

Blue Tango
Michael Van Walleghen (1989)

Eden
Dennis Schmitz (1989)

Waiting for Poppa at the Smith-
town Diner
Peter Serchuk (1990)

Great Blue
Brendan Galvin (1990)

What My Father Believed
Robert Wrigley (1991)

Something Grazes Our Hair
S. J. Marks (1991)

Walking the Blind Dog
G. E. Murray (1992)

The Sawdust War
Jim Barnes (1992)

The God of Indeterminacy
Sandra McPherson (1993)

Off-Season at the Edge of the
World
Debora Greger (1994)

Counting the Black Angels
Len Roberts (1994)

Oblivion
Stephen Berg (1995)

To Us, All Flowers Are Roses
Lorna Goodison (1995)

Honorable Amendments
Michael S. Harper (1995)

Points of Departure
Miller Williams (1995)

National Poetry Series

Eroding Witness
Nathaniel Mackey (1985)
Selected by Michael S. Harper

Palladium
Alice Fulton (1986)
Selected by Mark Strand

Cities in Motion
Sylvia Moss (1987)
Selected by Derek Walcott

The Hand of God and a Few
Bright Flowers
William Olsen (1988)
Selected by David Wagoner

The Great Bird of Love
Paul Zimmer (1989)
Selected by William Stafford

Stubborn
Roland Flint (1990)
Selected by Dave Smith

The Surface
Laura Mullen (1991)
Selected by C. K. Williams

The Dig
Lynn Emanuel (1992)
Selected by Gerald Stern

My Alexandria
Mark Doty (1993)
Selected by Philip Levine

The High Road to Taos
Martin Edmunds (1994)
Selected by Donald Hall

Theater of Animals
Samn Stockwell (1995)
Selected by Louise Glück

Other Poetry Volumes

Local Men and *Domains*
James Whitehead (1987)

Her Soul beneath the Bone:
Women's Poetry on Breast Cancer
Edited by Leatrice Lifshitz (1988)

Days from a Dream Almanac
Dennis Tedlock (1990)

Working Classics: Poems on
Industrial Life
*Edited by Peter Oresick and
Nicholas Coles* (1990)

Hummers, Knucklers, and Slow
Curves: Contemporary Baseball
Poems
Edited by Don Johnson (1991)

The Double Reckoning of
Christopher Columbus
Barbara Helfgott Hyett (1992)

Selected Poems
Jean Garrigue (1992)

New and Selected Poems,
1962–92
Laurence Lieberman (1993)

The Dig and *Hotel Fiesta*
Lynn Emanuel (1994)

For a Living: The Poetry of Work
*Edited by Nicholas Coles and Peter
Oresick* (1995)